Instructional Guides for Literature

Flora & Ulysses: The Illuminated Adventures

Based on the novel by Kate DiCamillo
Great Works Author: Debra J. Housel, M.A.

SHELL EDUCATION

Image Credits
Shutterstock (cover; pages 1, 11, 52, 65, 68)

Standards
© 2007 Teachers of English to Speakers of Other Languages, Inc. (TESOL)
© 2007 Board of Regents of the University of Wisconsin System. World-Class Instructional Design and Assessment (WIDA)
© Copyright 2010. National Governors Association Center for Best Practices and Council of Chief State School Officers. All rights reserved.

Shell Education
5301 Oceanus Drive
Huntington Beach, CA 92649-1030
http://www.shelleducation.com
ISBN 978-1-4807-8234-1
© 2015 Shell Educational Publishing, Inc.

The classroom teacher may reproduce copies of materials in this book for classroom use only. The reproduction of any part for an entire school or school system is strictly prohibited. No part of this publication may be transmitted, stored, or recorded in any form without written permission from the publisher.

Table of Contents

How to Use This Literature Guide 4
    Theme Thoughts 4
    Vocabulary 5
    Analyzing the Literature 6
    Reader Response 6
    Close Reading the Literature 6
    Making Connections 7
    Creating with the Story Elements 7
    Culminating Activity 8
    Comprehension Assessment 8
    Response to Literature 8

Correlation to the Standards 8
    Purpose and Intent of Standards 8
    How to Find Standards Correlations 8
    Standards Correlation Chart 9
    TESOL and WIDA Standards 10

About the Author—Kate DiCamillo 11
    Possible Texts for Text Comparisons 11
    Cross-Curricular Connection 11

Book Summary of *Flora & Ulysses: The Illuminated Adventures* 12
    Possible Texts for Text Sets 12

Teacher Plans and Student Pages 13
    Pre-Reading Theme Thoughts 13
    Section 1: Chapters 1–13 14
    Section 2: Chapters 14–26 24
    Section 3: Chapters 27–39 34
    Section 4: Chapters 40–52 44
    Section 5: Chapters 53–Epilogue 54

Post-Reading Activities 64
    Post-Reading Theme Thoughts 64
    Culminating Activity: Create a New Adventure! 65
    Comprehension Assessment 66
    Response to Literature: Caring For an Exotic Pet 68

Vocabulary List 69

Answer Key 71

How to Use This Literature Guide

Today's standards demand rigor and relevance in the reading of complex texts. The units in this series guide teachers in a rich and deep exploration of worthwhile works of literature for classroom study. The most rigorous instruction can also be interesting and engaging!

Many current strategies for effective literacy instruction have been incorporated into these instructional guides for literature. Throughout the units, text-dependent questions are used to determine comprehension of the book as well as student interpretation of the vocabulary words. The books chosen for the series are complex exemplars of carefully crafted works of literature. Close reading is used throughout the units to guide students toward revisiting the text and using textual evidence to respond to prompts orally and in writing. Students must analyze the story elements in multiple assignments for each section of the book. All of these strategies work together to rigorously guide students through their study of literature.

The next few pages will make clear how to use this guide for a purposeful and meaningful literature study. Each section of this guide is set up in the same way to make it easier for you to implement the instruction in your classroom.

Theme Thoughts

The great works of literature used throughout this series have important themes that have been relevant to people for many years. Many of the themes will be discussed during the various sections of this instructional guide. However, it would also benefit students to have independent time to think about the key themes of the novel.

Before students begin reading, have them complete *Pre-Reading Theme Thoughts* (page 13). This graphic organizer will allow students to think about the themes outside the context of the story. They'll have the opportunity to evaluate statements based on important themes and defend their opinions. Be sure to have students keep their papers for comparison to the *Post-Reading Theme Thoughts* (page 64). This graphic organizer is similar to the pre-reading activity. However, this time, students will be answering the questions from the point of view of one of the characters of the novel. They have to think about how the character would feel about each statement and defend their thoughts. To conclude the activity, have students compare what they thought about the themes before they read the novel to what the characters discovered during the story.

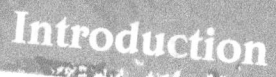

How to Use This Literature Guide (cont.)

Vocabulary

Each teacher overview page has definitions and sentences about how key vocabulary words are used in the section. These words should be introduced and discussed with students. There are two student vocabulary activity pages in each section. On the first page, students are asked to define the ten words chosen by the author of this unit. On the second page in most sections, each student will select at least eight words that he or she finds interesting or difficult. For each section, choose one of these pages for your students to complete. With either assignment, you may want to have students get into pairs to discuss the meanings of the words. Allow students to use reference guides to define the words. Monitor students to make sure the definitions they have found are accurate and relate to how the words are used in the text.

On some of the vocabulary student pages, students are asked to answer text-related questions about the vocabulary words. The following question stems will help you create your own vocabulary questions if you'd like to extend the discussion.

- How does this word describe _____'s character?
- In what ways does this word relate to the problem in this story?
- How does this word help you understand the setting?
- In what ways is this word related to the story's solution?
- Describe how this word supports the novel's theme of . . . .
- What visual images does this word bring to your mind?
- For what reasons might the author have chosen to use this particular word?

At times, more work with the words will help students understand their meanings. The following quick vocabulary activities are a good way to further study the words.

- Have students practice their vocabulary and writing skills by creating sentences and/or paragraphs in which multiple vocabulary words are used correctly and with evidence of understanding.
- Students can play vocabulary concentration. Students make a set of cards with the words and a separate set of cards with the definitions. Then, students lay the cards out on the table and play concentration. The goal of the game is to match vocabulary words with their definitions.
- Students can create word journal entries about the words. Students choose words they think are important and then describe why they think each word is important within the novel.

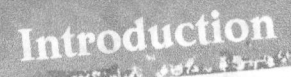

How to Use This Literature Guide (cont.)

Analyzing the Literature

After students have read each section, hold small-group or whole-class discussions. Questions are written at two levels of complexity to allow you to decide which questions best meet the needs of your students. The Level 1 questions are typically less abstract than the Level 2 questions. Level 1 is indicated by a square, while Level 2 is indicated by a triangle. These questions focus on the various story elements, such as character, setting, and plot. Student pages are provided if you want to assign these questions for individual student work before your group discussion. Be sure to add further questions as your students discuss what they've read. For each question, a few key points are provided for your reference as you discuss the novel with students.

Reader Response

In today's classrooms, there are often great readers who are below average writers. So much time and energy is spent in classrooms getting students to read on grade level, that little time is left to focus on writing skills. To help teachers include more writing in their daily literacy instruction, each section of this guide has a literature-based reader response prompt. Each of the three genres of writing is used in the reader responses within this guide: narrative, informative/explanatory, and argument. Students have a choice between two prompts for each reader response. One response requires students to make connections between the reading and their own lives. The other prompt requires students to determine text-to-text connections or connections within the text.

Close Reading the Literature

Within each section, students are asked to closely reread a short section of text. Since some versions of the novels have different page numbers, the selections are described by chapter and location, along with quotations to guide the readers. After each close reading, there are text-dependent questions to be answered by students.

Encourage students to read each question one at a time and then go back to the text and discover the answer. Work with students to ensure that they use the text to determine their answers rather than making unsupported inferences. Once students have answered the questions, discuss what they discovered. Suggested answers are provided in the answer key.

How to Use This Literature Guide (cont.)

Close Reading the Literature (cont.)

The generic, open-ended stems below can be used to write your own text-dependent questions if you would like to give students more practice.

- Give evidence from the text to support . . . .
- Justify your thinking using text evidence about . . . .
- Find evidence to support your conclusions about . . . .
- What text evidence helps the reader understand . . . ?
- Use the book to tell why _____ happens.
- Based on events in the story, ...
- Use text evidence to describe why . . . .

Making Connections

The activities in this section help students make cross-curricular connections to writing, mathematics, science, social studies, or the fine arts. Each of these types of activities requires higher-order thinking skills from students.

Creating with the Story Elements

It is important to spend time discussing the common story elements in literature. Understanding the characters, setting, and plot can increase students' comprehension and appreciation of the story. If teachers discuss these elements daily, students will more likely internalize the concepts and look for the elements in their independent reading. Another important reason for focusing on the story elements is that students will be better writers if they think about how the stories they read are constructed.

Students are given three options for working with the story elements. They are asked to create something related to the characters, setting, or plot of the novel. Students are given a choice on this activity so that they can decide to complete the activity that most appeals to them. Different multiple intelligences are used so that the activities are diverse and interesting to all students.

How to Use This Literature Guide (cont.)

Culminating Activity

This open-ended, cross-curricular activity requires higher-order thinking and allows for a creative product. Students will enjoy getting the chance to share what they have discovered through reading the novel. Be sure to allow them enough time to complete the activity at school or home.

Comprehension Assessment

The questions in this section are modeled after current standardized tests to help students analyze what they've read and prepare for tests they may see in their classrooms. The questions are dependent on the text and require critical-thinking skills to answer.

Response to Literature

The final post-reading activity is an essay based on the text that also requires further research by students. This is a great way to extend this book into other curricular areas. A suggested rubric is provided for teacher reference.

Correlation to the Standards

Shell Education is committed to producing educational materials that are research and standards based. As part of this effort, we have correlated all of our products to the academic standards of all 50 states, the District of Columbia, the Department of Defense Dependents Schools, and all Canadian provinces.

Purpose and Intent of Standards

Standards are designed to focus instruction and guide adoption of curricula. Standards are statements that describe the criteria necessary for students to meet specific academic goals. They define the knowledge, skills, and content students should acquire at each level. Standards are also used to develop standardized tests to evaluate students' academic progress. Teachers are required to demonstrate how their lessons meet standards. Standards are used in the development of all of our products, so educators can be assured they meet high academic standards.

How to Find Standards Correlations

To print a customized correlation report of this product for your state, visit our website at http://www.shelleducation.com and follow the online directions. If you require assistance in printing correlation reports, please contact our Customer Service Department at 1-877-777-3450.

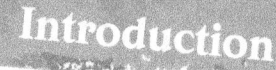

Correlation to the Standards (cont.)

Standards Correlation Chart

The lessons in this guide were written to support the Common Core College and Career Readiness Anchor Standards. This chart indicates which sections of this guide address the anchor standards.

Common Core College and Career Readiness Anchor Standard	Section
CCSS.ELA-Literacy.CCRA.R.1—Read closely to determine what the text says explicitly and to make logical inferences from it; cite specific textual evidence when writing or speaking to support conclusions drawn from the text.	Close Reading the Literature Sections 1–5; Analyzing the Literature Sections 1–5; Creating with the Story Elements Sections 1–5
CCSS.ELA-Literacy.CCRA.R.2—Determine central ideas or themes of a text and analyze their development; summarize the key supporting details and ideas.	Creating with the Story Elements Sections 1–5; Reader Response Sections 1–5; Post–Reading Theme Thoughts; Comprehension Assessment
CCSS.ELA-Literacy.CCRA.R.3—Analyze how and why individuals, events, or ideas develop and interact over the course of a text.	Analyzing the Literature Sections 1–5; Creating with the Story Elements Sections 1–5
CCSS.ELA-Literacy.CCRA.R.4—Interpret words and phrases as they are used in a text, including determining technical, connotative, and figurative meanings, and analyze how specific word choices shape meaning or tone.	Vocabulary Sections 1–5
CCSS.ELA-Literacy.CCRA.R.5—Analyze the structure of texts, including how specific sentences, paragraphs, and larger portions of the text (e.g., a section, chapter, scene, or stanza) relate to each other and the whole.	Close Reading the Literature Sections 1–5
CCSS.ELA-Literacy.CCRA.R.6—Assess how point of view or purpose shapes the content and style of a text.	Creating with the Story Elements Characters Section 4; Post–Reading Theme Thoughts
CCSS.ELA-Literacy.CCRA.R.7—Integrate and evaluate content presented in diverse media and formats, including visually and quantitatively, as well as in words.	Entire Unit
CCSS.ELA-Literacy.CCRA.R.10—Read and comprehend complex literary and informational texts independently and proficiently.	Entire Unit
CCSS.ELA-Literacy.CCRA.W.1—Write arguments to support claims in an analysis of substantive topics or texts using valid reasoning and relevant and sufficient evidence.	Close Reading the Literature Sections 1–5; Reader Response Sections 1, 4
CCSS.ELA-Literacy.CCRA.W.2—Write informative/explanatory texts to examine and convey complex ideas and information clearly and accurately through the effective selection, organization, and analysis of content.	Reader Response Sections 1, 3, 5; Making Connections Section 1; Making Connections Section 5; Post–Reading Response to Literature
CCSS.ELA-Literacy.CCRA.W.3—Write narratives to develop real or imagined experiences or events using effective technique, well-chosen details and well-structured event sequences.	Reader Response Sections 2–5; Creating with the Story Elements Sections 1–5

Correlation to the Standards (cont.)

Standards Correlation Chart (cont.)

Common Core College and Career Readiness Anchor Standard	Section
CCSS.ELA-Literacy.CCRA.W.4—Produce clear and coherent writing in which the development, organization, and style are appropriate to task, purpose, and audience.	Reader Response Sections 1–5; Creating with the Story Elements Sections 1–5; Making Connections Sections 1, 4–5; Post–Reading Response to Literature; Culminating Activity
CCSS.ELA-Literacy.CCRA.W.5—Develop and strengthen writing as needed by planning, revising, editing, rewriting, or trying a new approach.	Making Connections Sections 1, 4–5; Post-Reading Response to Literature; Culminating Activity
CCSS.ELA-Literacy.CCRA.W.6—Use technology, including the Internet, to produce and publish writing and to interact and collaborate with others.	Making Connections Sections 1, 4–5; Post-Reading Response to Literature
CCSS.ELA-Literacy.CCRA.W.7—Conduct short as well as more sustained research projects based on focused questions, demonstrating understanding of the subject under investigation.	Making Connections Sections 1, 4–5; Post-Reading Response to Literature
CCSS.ELA-Literacy.CCRA.W.8—Gather relevant information from multiple print and digital sources, assess the credibility and accuracy of each source, and integrate the information while avoiding plagiarism.	Making Connections Sections 1, 4–5; Creating with the Story Elements Section 3; Post-Reading Response to Literature
CCSS.ELA-Literacy.CCRA.L.1—Demonstrate command of the conventions of standard English grammar and usage when writing or speaking.	Reader Response Sections 1–5; Making Connections Sections 1–5
CCSS.ELA-Literacy.CCRA.L.2—Demonstrate command of the conventions of standard English capitalization, punctuation, and spelling when writing.	Reader Response Sections 1–5; Making Connections Sections 1–5; Post-Reading Response to Literature; Culminating Activity
CCSS.ELA-Literacy.CCRA.L.4—Determine or clarify the meaning of unknown and multiple-meaning words and phrases by using context clues, analyzing meaningful word parts, and consulting general and specialized reference materials, as appropriate.	Vocabulary Sections 1–5
CCSS.ELA-Literacy.CCRA.L.6—Acquire and use accurately a range of general academic and domain-specific words and phrases sufficient for reading, writing, speaking, and listening at the college and career readiness level; demonstrate independence in gathering vocabulary knowledge when encountering an unknown term important to comprehension or expression.	Vocabulary Sections 1–5

TESOL and WIDA Standards

The lessons in this book promote English language development for English language learners. The following TESOL and WIDA English Language Development Standards are addressed through the activities in this book:

- Standard 1: English language learners communicate for social and instructional purposes within the school setting.
- Standard 2: English language learners communicate information, ideas and concepts necessary for academic success in the content area of language arts.

About the Author—Kate DiCamillo

Kate DiCamillo was born in 1964 in Pennsylvania. She suffered from chronic pneumonia, so when she was 5, her family moved to Florida for the warm climate. Today she lives in Minnesota.

When she was 30 years old, DiCamillo became interested in writing for children while working in a book warehouse. Her dream came true when she became a children's fiction author in 2000 with the publication of *Because of Winn-Dixie*, a Newbery Honor book. She is one of very few authors to have her first novel named a Newbery Honor book. Since then, she has won the Newbery Award twice—once in 2003 for *The Tale of Despereaux* and again in 2014 for *Flora & Ulysses: The Illuminated Adventures*. She enjoys writing whimsical tales that feature talking animals.

DiCamillo writes two pages every weekday. Sometimes she uses the pages and other times she doesn't. However, she believes that writing is more discipline than talent, and thus writing daily is vital to hone her craft. It takes her approximately one year to write a novel.

The Library of Congress named DiCamillo the National Ambassador for Young People's Literature for the term 2014–2015. Many of DiCamillo's books have been made into movies.

Possible Texts for Text Comparisons

Kate DiCamillo is the author of *The Tale of Despereaux* (another Newbery Award winner), *Because of Winn-Dixie* (a Newbery Honor book), *The Miraculous Journey of Edward Tulane*, *The Tiger Rising*, *The Magician's Elephant*, and the *Mercy Watson* series.

Cross-Curricular Connection

This book can be used in a health unit that teaches CPR and the Heimlich maneuver or as part of a literature unit about graphic novels.

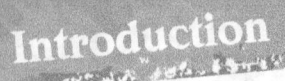

Book Summary of *Flora & Ulysses: The Illuminated Adventures*

Flora & Ulysses: The Illuminated Adventures has been heralded as a "genre-bending novel." It incorporates short written chapters with comic-strip chapters, creating a graphic novel within a novel.

The protagonist, ten-year-old Flora Belle Buckman, is a cynic. Her parents are divorced, and she believes her mother loves a pink shepherdess lamp more than her. She isolates herself from her parents and other children, spending all her time reading comic books about a superhero named Incandesto. All that changes when Tootie Tickham's husband gives her a vacuum cleaner that sucks up a squirrel. Flora does CPR to save the squirrel's life and discovers that being vacuumed has turned him into a superhero! She names him Ulysses after the name on the front of the vacuum.

Flora and Ulysses embark on a series of wacky adventures involving poetry, a donut restaurant, and a vicious cat. Flora's mother Phyllis becomes Ulysses's arch-nemesis, ordering Flora's father to put the "diseased" squirrel into a bag, hit him with a shovel, and bury him. When George Buckman fails to carry out her murderous mission, Phyllis takes matters into her own hands, absconding with Ulysses in the middle of the night.

Determined to save her squirrel, Flora enlists the help of a cast of oddball characters, including Tootie Tickham, her "temporarily blind" great-nephew William Spiver, and Dr. Meescham, an old woman from the mysterious land of Blundermeecen.

Through the strange twists and turns of the story, Flora tries to keep her cynical self from feeling emotions. However, she finds herself loving a furless squirrel, her lonely father, her grouchy mother, and the traumatized boy next door. Nearly every character in the story is unknowingly searching for love, and the reader is left believing that their search was not in vain.

Note: Part of the humor in this book relies on the use of words that are obscure and/or unusual for this reading level. Thus, a complete vocabulary list has been included on page 70 for your reference.

Possible Texts for Text Sets

- Dahl, Roald. *James and the Giant Peach*. Puffin, 2007.
- Dahl, Roald. *Matilda*. Puffin, 2007.
- Horvath, Polly. *Everything on a Waffle*. Square Fish, 2008.
- Horvath, Polly. *Mr. and Mrs. Bunny—Detectives Extraordinaire!* Schwartz & Wade, 2012.
- Horvath, Polly. *The Pepins and their Problems*. Square Fish, 2008.

Name _____

Date _____

Introduction

Pre-Reading Theme Thoughts

Directions: Read each statement in the first column. Decide if you agree or disagree with the statement. Record your opinion by marking an X in the Agree or Disagree column for each statement. Explain your choices in the fourth column. There are no right or wrong answers.

Statement	Agree	Disagree	Explain Your Answer
Most superheroes are created as the result of a near-tragic accident.			
Comics are the most entertaining type of literature.			
It is not wise to feel hopeful.			
Sometimes it's not clear that parents love their children.			

© Shell Education   #40111—Instructional Guide: Flora & Ulysses: The Illuminated Adventures

Teacher Plans—Section 1
Chapters 1–13

Vocabulary Overview

Ten key words from this section are provided below with definitions and sentences about how the words are used in the book. Choose one of the vocabulary activity sheets (pages 15 or 16) for students to complete as they read this section. Monitor students as they work to ensure the definitions they have found are accurate and relate to the text. Finally, discuss these important vocabulary words with students. If you think these words or other words in the section warrant more time devoted to them, there are suggestions in the introduction for other vocabulary activities (page 5).

Word	Definition	Sentence about Text
cynic (ch. 1)	one who believes that people are inherently selfish and only interested in helping themselves	Flora's mother says that her daughter is a natural-born **cynic**, and Flora believes her.
defiance (ch. 1)	a refusal to obey something or someone	Flora reads comic books in **defiance** of the contract her mother made her sign.
malfeasance (ch. 1)	wrongdoing or misconduct	Alfred T. Slipper, Flora's favorite comic book superhero, frequently says, "This **malfeasance** must be stopped."
profound (ch. 2)	showing great knowledge	Prior to being vacuumed, the squirrel's thoughts are all about finding food; his thinking is not **profound**.
indomitable (ch. 3)	impossible to defeat or discourage	Since it is **indomitable**, the Ulysses 2000X vacuum cleaner sucks up everything in its path.
inadvertently (ch. 4)	accidentally; unintentionally	Tootie **inadvertently** vacuums up a squirrel.
submersion (ch. 8)	completely under the surface of a liquid	Alfred T. Slipper becomes the Amazing Incandesto after he experiences **submersion** in a vat of cleaning solution.
disdain (ch. 8)	contempt; scorn	In the comic book, most people treat Alfred T. Slipper with **disdain**, not realizing that he's the Amazing Incandesto.
smirk (ch. 10)	to smile in an unpleasant way	Flora believes her mother's shepherdess lamp has a **smirk** on its face.
emblazoned (ch. 12)	clearly written or drawn on a surface	Flora envisions words **emblazoned** on the ceiling above her bed.

Name _____

Date _____

Chapters 1–13

Understanding Vocabulary Words

Directions: The following words appear in this section of the book. Use context clues and reference materials to determine an accurate definition for each word.

Word	Definition
cynic (ch. 1)	
defiance (ch. 1)	
malfeasance (ch. 1)	
profound (ch. 2)	
indomitable (ch. 3)	
inadvertently (ch. 4)	
submersion (ch. 8)	
disdain (ch. 8)	
smirk (ch. 10)	
emblazoned (ch. 12)	

Chapters 1–13

Name _____

Date _____

During-Reading Vocabulary Activity

Directions: As you read these chapters, record at least eight important words on the lines below. Try to find interesting, difficult, intriguing, special, or funny words. Your words can be long or short. They can be hard or easy to spell. After each word, use context clues in the text and reference materials to define the word.

- _____
- _____
- _____
- _____
- _____
- _____
- _____
- _____
- _____

Directions: Respond to these questions about the words in this section.

1. Why isn't typical squirrel **cogitation** considered **profound**?

   _____
   _____

2. Why are both the Amazing Incandesto and Ulysses described by Flora as **unassuming**?

   _____
   _____

Teacher Plans—Section 1
Chapters 1–13

Analyzing the Literature

Provided below are discussion questions you can use in small groups, with the whole class, or for written assignments. Each question is given at two levels so you can choose the right question for each group of students. Activity sheets with these questions are provided (pages 18–19) if you want students to write their responses. For each question, a few key discussion points are provided for your reference.

Story Element	■ Level 1	▲ Level 2	Key Discussion Points
Plot	How does Tootie Tickham's birthday gift set the plot in motion?	What does Tootie Tickham's husband do that sets up the events in the story?	For her birthday, Tootie's husband gives her a Ulysses 2000X vacuum cleaner and insists she try it out . . . in the backyard.
Character	What is Flora's relationship with her mother like, and how do you know?	Describe Flora's relationship with her mother.	Flora's relationship with her mother is strained. This is evident by the jealousy Flora shows regarding the shepherdess lamp and how she sneaks the squirrel past her mother.
Setting	How does the setting help make the story almost believable?	How does the setting draw in the reader and make the story seem almost real?	Flora is living in an ordinary house in an ordinary neighborhood until Tootie's vacuum cleaner sucks up a squirrel. The fact that everything is so ordinary until the extraordinary event makes the story more realistic.
Character	Does Flora's father live with her? Why or why not?	What do we know about Flora's father?	Flora's father doesn't live with Flora, as her parents are divorced. Flora's father tells Flora that her mother loved her romance novels instead of him.

Chapters 1–13

Name _____

Date _____

Analyzing the Literature

Directions: Think about the section you just read. Read each question and state your response with textual evidence.

1. How does Tootie Tickham's birthday gift set the plot in motion?

   _____
   _____
   _____
   _____

2. What is Flora's relationship with her mother like and how do you know?

   _____
   _____
   _____
   _____

3. How does the setting help make the story almost believable?

   _____
   _____
   _____
   _____

4. Does Flora's father live with her? Why or why not?

   _____
   _____
   _____
   _____

Name _____

Date _____

Chapters 1–13

▲ Analyzing the Literature

Directions: Think about the section you just read. Read each question and state your response with textual evidence.

1. What does Tootie Tickham's husband do that sets up the events in the story?

   _____
   _____
   _____
   _____

2. Describe Flora's relationship with her mother.

   _____
   _____
   _____
   _____

3. How does the setting draw in the reader and make the story seem almost real?

   _____
   _____
   _____
   _____

4. What do we know about Flora's father?

   _____
   _____
   _____
   _____

Chapters 1–13

Name _____

Date _____

Reader Response

Directions: Choose one of the following prompts about this section to answer. Be sure you include a topic sentence in your response, use textual evidence to support your opinion, and provide a strong conclusion that summarizes your opinion.

Writing Prompts

- **Informative/Explanatory Piece**—Flora's hobby is reading the *Illuminated Adventures of the Amazing Incandesto!* and *TERRIBLE THINGS CAN HAPPEN TO YOU!* She frequently refers to knowledge she's gained from her reading of these books. Describe a hobby that you enjoy and what you've learned from it.
- **Opinion/Argument Piece**—Why did the author choose to have Ulysses become a superhero after being vacuumed? Was this a wise choice? Explain your response.

_____
_____
_____
_____
_____
_____
_____
_____
_____
_____
_____
_____
_____

Name _____

Date _____

Chapters 1–13

Close Reading the Literature

Directions: Closely reread the page in chapter 10 where Flora thinks about the first time she saw Mary Ann, the shepherdess lamp. Start reading with, "Her mother had sent away . . . ." Stop reading at the end of the chapter. Read each question and then revisit the text to find evidence that supports your answer.

1. What does Flora's mother say about Mary Ann when she first arrives?

   _____
   _____
   _____

2. What is Flora's opinion of Mary Ann? Give examples from the text.

   _____
   _____
   _____
   _____
   _____

3. Find evidence in the text that supports whether or not Flora is jealous of Mary Ann.

   _____
   _____
   _____

4. How do you know that Flora already cares more for Ulysses than she ever has for Mary Ann?

   _____
   _____
   _____
   _____

Chapters 1–13

Name _____

Date _____

Making Connections–Learning About CPR/the Heimlich Maneuver

> Flora uses CPR to revive Ulysses after his encounter with the vacuum cleaner. She learned to do CPR from reading TERRIBLE THINGS CAN HAPPEN TO YOU! In another issue of the same comic, she learned about doing the Heimlich maneuver.

Directions: Choose CPR (cardiopulmonary resuscitation) or the Heimlich maneuver. Do research to learn more about your choice. Then, answer the questions below.

1. What is the purpose of this technique?

    _____
    _____

2. When should this technique be used?

    _____

3. List the steps in order. Include all essential information:

    - _____
    - _____
    - _____
    - _____
    - _____

4. How does one know if the technique is successful?

    _____
    _____

Name _____

Date _____

Chapters 1–13

Creating with the Story Elements

Directions: Thinking about the story elements of character, setting, and plot in a novel is very important to understanding what is happening and why. Complete **one** of the following activities based on what you've read so far. Be creative and have fun!

Characters

Draw a picture showing Flora resuscitating Ulysses after Tootie vacuums him. Refer back to the book to include many details.

Setting

Make a map of the Buckmans' and Tickhams' backyards and homes. Use information from the text to label your map carefully with important locations of events in the story.

Plot

Some of the events in this story are facts; others are clearly fiction because they couldn't really happen. Reproduce the graphic organizer below. Under the title **Fact**, write the events that are real. Under the title **Fiction**, write the events that are made up.

Fact	Fiction

Teacher Plans—Section 2
Chapters 14–26

Vocabulary Overview

Ten key words from this section are provided below with definitions and sentences about how the words are used in the book. Choose one of the vocabulary activity sheets (pages 25 or 26) for students to complete as they read this section. Monitor students as they work to ensure the definitions they have found are accurate and relate to the text. Finally, discuss these important vocabulary words with students. If you think these words or other words in the section warrant more time devoted to them, there are suggestions in the introduction for other vocabulary activities (page 5).

Word	Definition	Sentence about Text
stout (ch. 14)	having a large, wide body	Flora's mother accuses her of eating a whole bag of cheese puffs and warns that she'll become **stout**.
plastered (ch. 16)	used figuratively to mean "painted on"	Flora's mother Phyllis **plasters** a fake smile on her face.
dictums (ch. 17)	well-known sayings that state important ideas or rules	*The Criminal Element Is Among Us* offers **dictums** about identifying potential criminals.
induced (ch. 17)	caused	William Spiver states that his temporary blindness was **induced** by a trauma.
anticlimactic (ch. 18)	something that is much less exciting or dramatic than had been anticipated	Flora feels that having a superhero squirrel is **anticlimactic** when he doesn't immediately start vanquishing villains.
cryptic (ch. 18)	seeming to have a hidden meaning	When William won't tell Flora why he became blind, she says he is being **cryptic**.
arch-nemesis (ch. 21)	most significant enemy	Flora initially worries that Ulysses's **arch-nemesis** might be William Spiver.
neurotic (ch. 25)	always fearful or worried about something	Great-Aunt Tootie refers to William Spiver as **neurotic** because she thinks he is pretending to be blind.
hyperbole (ch. 25)	an obvious, extravagant exaggeration	William uses **hyperbole** when he states that his dark glasses have been glued to his head by evil forces.
obfuscation (ch. 26)	making something hard to understand	Flora starts planning **obfuscation** in the hopes of preventing Ulysses from being killed by her father.

Name _____

Date _____

Chapters 14–26

Understanding Vocabulary Words

Directions: The following words appear in this section of the book. Use context clues and reference materials to determine an accurate definition for each word.

Word	Definition
stout (ch. 14)	
plastered (ch. 16)	
dictums (ch. 17)	
induced (ch. 17)	
anticlimactic (ch. 18)	
cryptic (ch. 18)	
arch-nemesis (ch. 21)	
neurotic (ch. 25)	
hyperbole (ch. 25)	
obfuscation (ch. 26)	

Chapters 14–26

Name _____

Date _____

During-Reading Vocabulary Activity

Directions: As you read these chapters, record at least eight important words on the lines below. Try to find interesting, difficult, intriguing, special, or funny words. Your words can be long or short. They can be hard or easy to spell. After each word, use context clues in the text and reference materials to define the word.

- _____
- _____
- _____
- _____
- _____
- _____
- _____
- _____
- _____

Directions: Respond to these questions about the words in this section.

1. Why is Phyllis convinced that Ulysses is **rabid**?

   _____
   _____

2. What kind of noise does Flora's home doorbell **emit**?

   _____
   _____

Teacher Plans—Section 2
Chapters 14–26

Analyzing the Literature

Provided below are discussion questions you can use in small groups, with the whole class, or for written assignments. Each question is given at two levels so you can choose the right question for each group of students. Activity sheets with these questions are provided (pages 28–29) if you want students to write their responses. For each question, a few key discussion points are provided for your reference.

Story Element	■ Level 1	▲ Level 2	Key Discussion Points
Plot	What does Phyllis tell George to do with the squirrel?	Phyllis outlines a plan of action for George to take with Ulysses. Why does she make this plan?	Phyllis wants George to put the squirrel inside a sack and hit him with a shovel, then use the shovel to dig a hole and bury the dead animal. She doesn't want her daughter hanging out with a "rabid" squirrel.
Character	Why is what Ulysses wrote on the computer more significant than what he wrote on the typewriter?	What aspects of Ulysses writing on the computer make it more compelling than when he wrote on the typewriter?	Ulysses wrote on the typewriter in the middle of the night. Nobody was there, and no one can swear that he wrote it. The writing he does on the computer is done in front of Tootie, William, and Flora, so they know for sure that he did it.
Setting	What does the description of Flora's doorbell ringing tell the reader about her home?	Explain how the sound of Flora's doorbell compares with her feelings about her home.	Flora does not feel her home is a loving, warm, welcoming place. Her doorbell sounds jarring and discordant, which fits with her negative view.
Character	Why does William Spiver ask Flora if she will return?	Why is it important to William Spiver that Flora return home after visiting her father?	William Spiver really wants Flora to return and is seeking her reassurance. Although they don't know each other well, he seems to have already become attached to her.

Chapters 14–26

Name _____

Date _____

Analyzing the Literature

Directions: Think about the section you just read. Read each question and state your response with textual evidence.

1. What does Phyllis tell George to do with the squirrel?

   _____
   _____
   _____
   _____

2. Why is what Ulysses wrote on the computer more significant than what he wrote on the typewriter?

   _____
   _____
   _____
   _____

3. What does the description of Flora's doorbell ringing tell the reader about her home?

   _____
   _____
   _____
   _____

4. Why does William Spiver ask Flora if she will return?

   _____
   _____
   _____
   _____

Name _____

Date _____

Chapters 14–26

▲ Analyzing the Literature

Directions: Think about the section you just read. Read each question and state your response with textual evidence.

1. Phyllis outlines a plan of action for George to take with Ulysses. Why does she make this plan?

   _____
   _____
   _____
   _____

2. What aspects of Ulysses writing on the computer make it more compelling than when he wrote on the typewriter?

   _____
   _____
   _____
   _____

3. Explain how the sound of Flora's doorbell compares with her feelings about her home.

   _____
   _____
   _____

4. Why is it important to William Spiver that Flora return home after visiting her father?

   _____
   _____
   _____

Chapters 14–26

Name _____

Date _____

Reader Response

Directions: Choose one of the following prompts about this section to answer. Be sure you include a topic sentence in your response, use textual evidence to support your opinion, and provide a strong conclusion that summarizes your opinion.

Writing Prompts

- **Opinion/Argument Piece**—You have the opportunity to spend a weekend with one of the book's characters. Who would you choose and why?
- **Narrative Piece**—George Buckman has the strange habit of introducing himself over and over again to people. In what ways does this strange habit of his make him a more likeable character?

_____
_____
_____
_____
_____
_____
_____
_____
_____
_____
_____
_____
_____

Name _____
Date _____

Chapters 14–26

Close Reading the Literature

Directions: Closely reread chapter 17 when Flora first meets William Spiver. Read each question and then revisit the text to find evidence that supports your answer.

1. Describe what happens to William on his way walking over to Flora's house.

   _____
   _____
   _____
   _____

2. Using evidence from the text, explain how you know that Phyllis is glad that William Spiver has come to spend the summer at the Tickhams' house.

   _____
   _____
   _____

3. Based on Flora's reaction, how does she feel about William Spiver spending the summer at the Tickhams' house?

   _____
   _____
   _____

4. According to the text, what makes Flora feel confident stating that she is not strange?

   _____
   _____
   _____

Chapters 14–26

Name _____

Date _____

Making Connections–Rilke Poetry

Directions: In chapter 25, Tootie reads aloud to Ulysses a poem written by Rainer Maria Rilke, a German poet. One of Rilke's earliest poems is printed below. Read this poem and reread the poem in the book. Then, use Rilke's style of writing to write a poem of your own.

Evening

By Rainer Maria Rilke

The bleak fields are asleep,
My heart alone wakes;
The evening in the harbour
Down his red sails takes.

Night, guardian of dreams,
Now wanders through the land;
The moon, a lily white,
Blossoms within her hand.

_____
_____
_____
_____
_____
_____
_____
_____
_____
_____
_____
_____
_____
_____
_____
_____
_____
_____
_____
_____

Name _____

Date _____

Chapters 14–26

Creating with the Story Elements

Directions: Thinking about the story elements of character, setting, and plot in a novel is very important to understanding what is happening and why. Complete **one** of the following activities based on what you've read so far. Be creative and have fun!

Characters

Choose a character. Draw, trace, or photocopy the character's image. Mount the image in the center of a character wheel like the one below. In each space on the wheel, write adjectives and/or phrases describing six of the character's personality traits. Be ready to defend your choices.

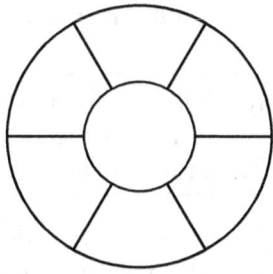

Setting

Draw a color picture of the Tickhams and Flora as they walk around the backyard "returning Ulysses to the wild." Be sure to include small details, like Tootie's gloves.

Plot

Think about Flora's father. What role do you think he will play as this book continues? Make a T-chart. On one side, list details that suggest he might help Flora's mother. On the other side, list details that suggest he might help Flora and Ulysses.

Teacher Plans—Section 3
Chapters 27–39

Vocabulary Overview

Ten key words from this section are provided below with definitions and sentences about how the words are used in the book. Choose one of the vocabulary activity sheets (pages 35 or 36) for students to complete as they read this section. Monitor students as they work to ensure the definitions they have found are accurate and relate to the text. Finally, discuss these important vocabulary words with students. If you think these words or other words in the section warrant more time devoted to them, there are suggestions in the introduction for other vocabulary activities (page 5).

Word	Definition	Sentence about Text
nefarious (ch. 28)	evil; immoral	Flora worries that her mother has convinced her father to do a **nefarious** deed.
surreptitiously (ch. 29)	secretly; stealthily	Flora **surreptitiously** removes the lid from the shoe box so that Ulysses can see what is happening inside the restaurant.
preternaturally (ch. 33)	unnaturally; seemingly conflicts with nature	After Ulysses causes a huge commotion in the restaurant, there is a moment that is **preternaturally** calm.
imperative (ch. 34)	very important	It is **imperative** that the Buckmans and their squirrel escape from the Giant Do-Nut.
notorious (ch. 34)	famous for doing something wrong or negative; infamous	Mr. Klaus the cat is **notorious** for attacking the apartment building's residents.
perpetual (ch. 35)	continuing forever	The apartment building's hallway is lit with **perpetual** green twilight.
mesmerizing (ch. 37)	so amazing that it demands one's complete attention	Ulysses finds gazing into Dr. Meescham's eye **mesmerizing**.
dilated (ch. 37)	enlarged	Ulysses's eyes are not **dilated**, which is a sign that he probably doesn't have a concussion.
conjured (ch. 38)	brought an image into someone's mind	Hearing Dr. Meescham's words **conjures** up the face of William Spiver for Flora.
inconsequential (ch. 38)	unimportant; irrelevant	Dr. Meescham tells Flora that in Blundermeecen girls were expected to talk about **inconsequential** things.

Name _____

Date _____

Chapters 27–39

Understanding Vocabulary Words

Directions: The following words appear in this section of the book. Use context clues and reference materials to determine an accurate definition for each word.

Word	Definition
nefarious (ch. 28)	
surreptitiously (ch. 29)	
preternaturally (ch. 33)	
imperative (ch. 34)	
notorious (ch. 34)	
perpetual (ch. 35)	
mesmerizing (ch. 37)	
dilated (ch. 37)	
conjured (ch. 38)	
inconsequential (ch. 38)	

© Shell Education   #40111—Instructional Guide: Flora & Ulysses: The Illuminated Adventures   35

Chapters 27–39

Name _____

Date _____

During-Reading Vocabulary Activity

Directions: As you read these chapters, record at least eight important words on the lines below. Try to find interesting, difficult, intriguing, special, or funny words. Your words can be long or short. They can be hard or easy to spell. After each word, use context clues in the text and reference materials to define the word.

- _____
- _____
- _____
- _____
- _____
- _____
- _____
- _____
- _____
- _____

Directions: Now, organize your words. Rewrite each of the words on a sticky note. Work with a group to create a bar graph of your words. Stack any words that are the same on top of one another. Different words should appear in different columns. Finally, discuss with the group why certain words were chosen more often than other words.

Teacher Plans—Section 3
Chapters 27–39

Analyzing the Literature

Provided below are discussion questions you can use in small groups, with the whole class, or for written assignments. Each question is given at two levels so you can choose the right question for each group of students. Activity sheets with these questions are provided (pages 38–39) if you want students to write their responses. For each question, a few key discussion points are provided for your reference.

Story Element	■ Level 1	▲ Level 2	Key Discussion Points
Character	How does Ulysses react when Rita discovers him?	What does Rita do that incites Ulysses into action?	Rita pokes her pencil into the shoe box, and when she sees Ulysses, she screams. This terrifies him, and he leaps out of the box and into her hair.
Plot	What happens after the Buckmans leave the restaurant?	Where do the Buckmans escape to after the commotion in the restaurant?	The Buckmans grab the unconscious Ulysses and run to their car. They then make a slow getaway (Mr. Buckman never speeds) to George Buckman's apartment.
Setting	Does George Buckman's apartment building seem like a nice place to live? Why or why not?	How do you know that the Blixen Arms is not a warm and welcoming place to live?	George Buckman's apartment building is gloomy with hallways lit in "perpetual green twilight." Worst of all is Mr. Klaus, a large, angry cat that makes life miserable for the residents by peeing on their doors, vomiting in the stairwells, and attacking them as they walk by.
Character	What are some unusual things Dr. Meescham says about her childhood in Blundermeecen?	Describe at least two unusual memories Dr. Meescham has from growing up in Blundermeecen.	In Blundermeecen, the words on the sign are often false, people are often getting concussions as gifts from the trolls, young girls knit outfits for the trolls, and the people are always anticipating a miracle.

Chapters 27–39

Name _____

Date _____

Analyzing the Literature

Directions: Think about the section you just read. Read each question and state your response with textual evidence.

1. How does Ulysses react when Rita discovers him?

   _____
   _____
   _____
   _____

2. What happens after the Buckmans leave the restaurant?

   _____
   _____
   _____
   _____

3. Does George Buckman's apartment building seem like a nice place to live? Why or why not?

   _____
   _____
   _____
   _____

4. What are some unusual things Dr. Meescham says about her childhood in Blundermeecen?

   _____
   _____
   _____

Name _____

Date _____

Chapters 27–39

▲ Analyzing the Literature

Directions: Think about the section you just read. Read each question and state your response with textual evidence.

1. What does Rita do that incites Ulysses into action?

   _____
   _____
   _____
   _____

2. Where do the Buckmans escape to after the commotion in the restaurant?

   _____
   _____
   _____
   _____

3. How do you know that the Blixen Arms is not a warm and welcoming place to live?

   _____
   _____
   _____
   _____

4. Describe at least two unusual memories Dr. Meescham has from growing up in Blundermeecen.

   _____
   _____
   _____
   _____

Chapters 27–39

Name _____

Date _____

Reader Response

Directions: Choose one of the following prompts about this section to answer. Be sure you include a topic sentence in your response, use textual evidence to support your opinion, and provide a strong conclusion that summarizes your opinion.

Writing Prompts

- **Narrative Piece**—How does your life compare to Flora's life? What are some things you have in common? What are some differences?
- **Informative/Explanatory Piece**—What questions are forming in your mind about the characters at this point? Write at least two questions and explain why you are curious about the answers.

Name _____

Date _____

Close Reading the Literature

Chapters 27–39

Directions: Closely reread the section in chapter 39 beginning with, "I'm a cynic!" Read to the end of the chapter. Read each question and then revisit the text to find evidence that supports your answer.

1. How does Dr. Meescham respond to Flora's announcement that she's a cynic?

   _____
   _____
   _____
   _____

2. What does Dr. Meescham say that prompts Flora to reveal to her that the squirrel is a superhero?

   _____
   _____
   _____

3. Flora expresses disappointment because Ulysses hasn't behaved like a typical superhero. Does Dr. Meescham agree? Use words from the text in your response.

   _____
   _____
   _____

4. Use text evidence to support the idea that Dr. Meescham is an optimist.

   _____
   _____
   _____
   _____

Chapters 27–39

Name _____

Date _____

Making Connections—Exclamation Marks

Directions: Read Flora's accurate explanation of when exclamation marks should be used at the beginning of chapter 36. Then, read each sentence below. Determine whether it should end with a period, an exclamation mark, or a question mark. Put the correct punctuation mark(s) in the space(s) provided. Explain your choice. The first one is done for you.

Insert the Punctuation Mark(s)	Tell Why You Chose It
Example "Does rabies itch _?_" asked Flora's father _._	The spoken sentence asks a question. The full sentence is a statement and needs a period.
1. "Help me _____" screamed Rita _____	
2. Ernie and Rita work at the Giant Do-Nut _____	
3. "Ulysses _____" Flora shouted to him _____	
4. Is that a rabid animal _____	
5. "For the love of Pete, what's so funny _____"	
6. Get out of the way _____	
7. Dr. Meescham lives in the Blixen Arms building _____	
8. The giant squid is a lonely creature _____	
9. "Holy bagumba _____"	
10. Why does Flora slide off the horsehair sofa _____	

42   #40111—Instructional Guide: Flora & Ulysses: The Illuminated Adventures   © Shell Education

Name _____

Date _____

Chapters 27–39

Creating with the Story Elements

Directions: Thinking about the story elements of character, setting, and plot in a novel is very important to understanding what is happening and why. Complete **one** of the following activities based on what you've read so far. Be creative and have fun!

Characters

Rita the waitress fears that she caught rabies from Ulysses being in her hair. Use the following website to conduct some research. Then, write an email to Rita explaining why she should or should not be worried.

- Visit the *Centers for Disease Control and Prevention* website (www.cdc.gov).
- Click on **CDC A–Z INDEX**.
- Choose **R**.
- Then, choose **Rabies**.
- Finally, choose **What is the risk for my pet?**

Setting

Make a cutaway model of the Blixen Arms hallway that includes Dr. Meescham's and George Buckman's apartments. A cutaway model has one wall removed so that the inside layout and details can be seen. You can create a drawing, a computer model, or a three-dimensional version.

Plot

Create a travel brochure for Blundermeecen based on ideas from Dr. Meescham's memories of the place. What would the homes and countryside look like? What kinds of things would tourists see there?

© Shell Education   #40111—Instructional Guide: Flora & Ulysses: The Illuminated Adventures   43

Teacher Plans—Section 4
Chapters 40–52

Vocabulary Overview

Ten key words from this section are provided below with definitions and sentences about how the words are used in the book. Choose one of the vocabulary activity sheets (pages 45 or 46) for students to complete as they read this section. Monitor students as they work to ensure the definitions they have found are accurate and relate to the text. Finally, discuss these important vocabulary words with students. If you think these words or other words in the section warrant more time devoted to them, there are suggestions in the introduction for other vocabulary activities (page 5).

Word	Definition	Sentence about Text
palpable (ch. 42)	noticeable; easily perceptible	George Buckman's fear of Mr. Klaus the cat is **palpable**.
treacherous (ch. 44)	unable to be trusted	Flora feels that her own heart is **treacherous** because it leaps with delight when she sees William.
persevere (ch. 45)	to continue trying to do something even though it is hard to do	William Spiver **perseveres** in helping Phyllis write her romance novel.
manifestations (ch. 45)	clear, obvious signs	The **manifestation** of William Spiver's banishment is his blindness.
appellation (ch. 48)	name	William Spiver strongly dislikes the **appellation** Billy.
irrevocable (ch. 48)	incapable of being changed; impossible to undo	William Spiver feels that what he did to his stepfather has caused an **irrevocable** rift in their relationship.
fraught (ch. 48)	full of; loaded	William Spiver is **fraught** with grief over the death of his father.
coherence (ch. 50)	having the quality of being logical, well-organized, and easy to understand	Only the last lines of Ulysses's "poem" have **coherence**; the rest is actually just a list of things he wants to write about.
vehemently (ch. 51)	intensely angry or emotional	Flora does not argue **vehemently** about where the squirrel should sit during dinner.
sentiments (ch. 51)	attitudes or opinions	During dinner, Flora's mother is acting strangely; she is not expressing her typical **sentiments**.

Name _____

Date _____

Chapters 40–52

Understanding Vocabulary Words

Directions: The following words appear in this section of the book. Use context clues and reference materials to determine an accurate definition for each word.

Word	Definition
palpable (ch. 42)	
treacherous (ch. 44)	
persevere (ch. 45)	
manifestations (ch. 45)	
appellation (ch. 48)	
irrevocable (ch. 48)	
fraught (ch. 48)	
coherence (ch. 50)	
vehemently (ch. 51)	
sentiments (ch. 51)	

Chapters 40–52

Name _____

Date _____

During-Reading Vocabulary Activity

Directions: As you read these chapters, record at least eight important words on the lines below. Try to find interesting, difficult, intriguing, special, or funny words. Your words can be long or short. They can be hard or easy to spell. After each word, use context clues in the text and reference materials to define the word.

- _____
- _____
- _____
- _____
- _____
- _____
- _____
- _____
- _____
- _____
- _____

Directions: Respond to these questions about the words in this section.

1. Why does seeing her home cause Flora a feeling of **foreboding**?
   _____
   _____

2. Who **banished** William Spiver and why?
   _____
   _____

Analyzing the Literature

Provided below are discussion questions you can use in small groups, with the whole class, or for written assignments. Each question is given at two levels so you can choose the right question for each group of students. Activity sheets with these questions are provided (pages 48–49) if you want students to write their responses. For each question, a few key discussion points are provided for your reference.

Story Element	■ Level 1	▲ Level 2	Key Discussion Points
Character	Describe how Ulysses saves George Buckman.	Who does Ulysses vanquish and how does he do it?	Mr. Klaus the cat lands on top of George Buckman's head. Ulysses flies through the air, grabs the cat, and throws him down the hall. The cat lands against the wall in a heap.
Plot	Tell how Flora's feelings about William Spiver have changed.	How has Flora's attitude toward William Spiver altered in a matter of hours?	William is "growing on" Flora. When she left home, she told her father not to stop the car so William could speak to her. When she returns home, she finds herself happy that William is there. In fact, her heart leaps when she sees him.
Setting	How does Ulysses get down to the kitchen when Flora's bedroom door is closed?	How does Ulysses "defeat" the closed bedroom door?	Ulysses flies through the air and lands on the door handle. His weight makes the handle move, so the door opens. Then he runs/flies through the house to the kitchen.
Character	How does Flora feel when her mother agrees to let her live with her father?	When Flora announces she wants to live with her father, how does she feel about her mother's reaction?	When Flora asks to live with her father, Phyllis responds with, "Go ahead; it would make my life easier." Flora feels as if each of her mother's words are enormous slabs of stone that are striking her and knocking her sideways.

Chapters 40–52

Name _____

Date _____

Analyzing the Literature

Directions: Think about the section you just read. Read each question and state your response with textual evidence.

1. Describe how Ulysses saves George Buckman.

   _____
   _____
   _____
   _____

2. Tell how Flora's feelings about William Spiver have changed.

   _____
   _____
   _____
   _____

3. How does Ulysses get down to the kitchen when Flora's bedroom door is closed?

   _____
   _____
   _____
   _____

4. How does Flora feel when her mother agrees to let her live with her father?

   _____
   _____
   _____
   _____

Name _____
Date _____

Chapters 40–52

▲ Analyzing the Literature

Directions: Think about the section you just read. Read each question and state your response with textual evidence.

1. Who does Ulysses vanquish and how does he do it?

   _____
   _____
   _____
   _____

2. How has Flora's attitude toward William Spiver altered in a matter of hours?

   _____
   _____
   _____
   _____

3. How does Ulysses "defeat" the closed bedroom door?

   _____
   _____
   _____
   _____

4. When Flora announces she wants to live with her father, how does she feel about her mother's reaction?

   _____
   _____
   _____
   _____

Chapters 40–52

Name _____

Date _____

Reader Response

Directions: Choose one of the following prompts about this section to answer. Be sure you include a topic sentence in your response, use textual evidence to support your opinion, and provide a strong conclusion that summarizes your opinion.

Writing Prompts
- **Narrative Piece**—Describe a few real-life people or events that you are reminded of by the characters and/or events in this story.
- **Opinion/Argument Piece**—What "irrevocable acts" do you think William Spiver committed that caused his mother to banish him to his Great Aunt Tootie's house? Explain why you think he did these things.

Name _____

Date _____

Chapters 40–52

Close Reading the Literature

Directions: Closely reread all of chapter 48. Read each question and then revisit the text to find evidence that supports your answer.

1. Why does Flora tell William that her mother wants her to move out? Does William agree?

   _____
   _____
   _____
   _____

2. According to the text, what does the word *banished* feel like to Flora? Why?

   _____
   _____
   _____

3. Use words from the text to describe William Spiver's father.

   _____
   _____
   _____

4. What three things about Tyrone really bother William? Cite evidence from the text.

   _____
   _____
   _____
   _____

Chapters 40–52

Name _____

Date _____

Making Connections–Quarks, Dwarf Stars, and Black Holes

Directions: William Spiver states that his interests include quarks, dwarf stars, and black holes, all phenomena that are a part of our expanding universe. Choose one of these phenomena and conduct research on it using books, magazine articles, videos, and/or the Internet. Then, write a few paragraphs about what you learned. You may want to include a drawing or an image from the Internet on another piece of paper.

_____
_____
_____
_____
_____
_____
_____
_____
_____
_____
_____
_____
_____
_____
_____
_____
_____

Name _____

Date _____

Chapters 40–52

Creating with the Story Elements

Directions: Thinking about the story elements of character, setting, and plot in a novel is very important to understanding what is happening and why. Complete **one** of the following activities based on what you've read so far. Be creative and have fun!

Characters

Giving 360-degree feedback means looking at something from all sides. Do a 360-profile on William Spiver. Write short descriptions of William from the points of view of these characters: Phyllis Buckman, Flora Buckman, and Tootie Tickham.

Setting

Draw a picture showing Flora, Phyllis, and Ulysses having dinner together. Use information from the text to make the picture as accurate as possible.

Plot

Write a letter from Flora to her mother explaining why "this malfeasance must be stopped" regarding Phyllis's plans for Ulysses.

Teacher Plans—Section 5
Chapters 53–Epilogue

Vocabulary Overview

Key words from this section are provided below with definitions and sentences about how the words are used in the book. Choose one of the vocabulary activity sheets (pages 55 or 56) for students to complete as they read this section. Monitor students as they work to ensure the definitions they have found are accurate and relate to the text. Finally, discuss these important vocabulary words with students. If you think these words or other words in the section warrant more time devoted to them, there are suggestions in the introduction for other vocabulary activities (page 5).

Word	Definition	Sentence about Text
provoke (ch. 52)	caused to be angry or violent	When Ulysses types on Phyllis's typewriter, it **provokes** her.
depleted (ch. 55)	emptied	After Ulysses types the lies that Phyllis demands he write, he feels **depleted**.
appalled (ch. 59)	felt fear, shock, or disgust	George Buckman would be **appalled** by the way that Tootie Tickham drives.
pervasive (ch. 60)	existing in or spreading through every part of something	Ulysses is frightened in the woods by the **pervasive** scent of raccoon.
sinkhole (ch. 61)	a low-lying depression; a hole in the ground that forms when a large amount of dirt and rocks are removed	William Spiver says that he deliberately drove his stepfather's truck into a **sinkhole**.
incandescent (ch. 61)	white or glowing due to great heat	William Spiver tells Flora that he was blinded by his mother's **incandescent** rage.
digress (ch. 63)	to speak off-topic; to talk about something other than the main subject of a discussion	Dr. Meescham **digresses** when she is talking to Ulysses.
inexplicable (ch. 64)	unable to be explained	As the trio walks along the highway, they encounter a lot of **inexplicable** litter strewn beside the road.
sepulchral (ch. 65)	very dismal or gloomy; like a tomb	William Spiver says that even the **sepulchral** gloom of the Blixen Arms cannot dim the beauty of Flora's face.
emanated (ch. 66)	came from a source	A fishy smell **emanates** from Ulysses's whiskers after he eats the sardines.

Name _____

Date _____

Chapters 53–Epilogue

Understanding Vocabulary Words

Directions: The following words appear in this section of the book. Use context clues and reference materials to determine an accurate definition for each word.

Word	Definition
provoke (ch. 52)	
depleted (ch. 55)	
appalled (ch. 59)	
pervasive (ch. 60)	
sinkhole (ch. 61)	
incandescent (ch. 61)	
digress (ch. 63)	
inexplicable (ch. 64)	
sepulchral (ch. 65)	
emanated (ch. 66)	

Chapters 53–Epilogue

Name _____

Date _____

During-Reading Vocabulary Activity

Directions: As you read these chapters, choose five important words from the story. Use these words to complete the word flow chart below. On each arrow, write a word. In each box, explain how the connected pair of words relates to each other. An example for the words *sinkhole* and *incandescent* has been done for you.

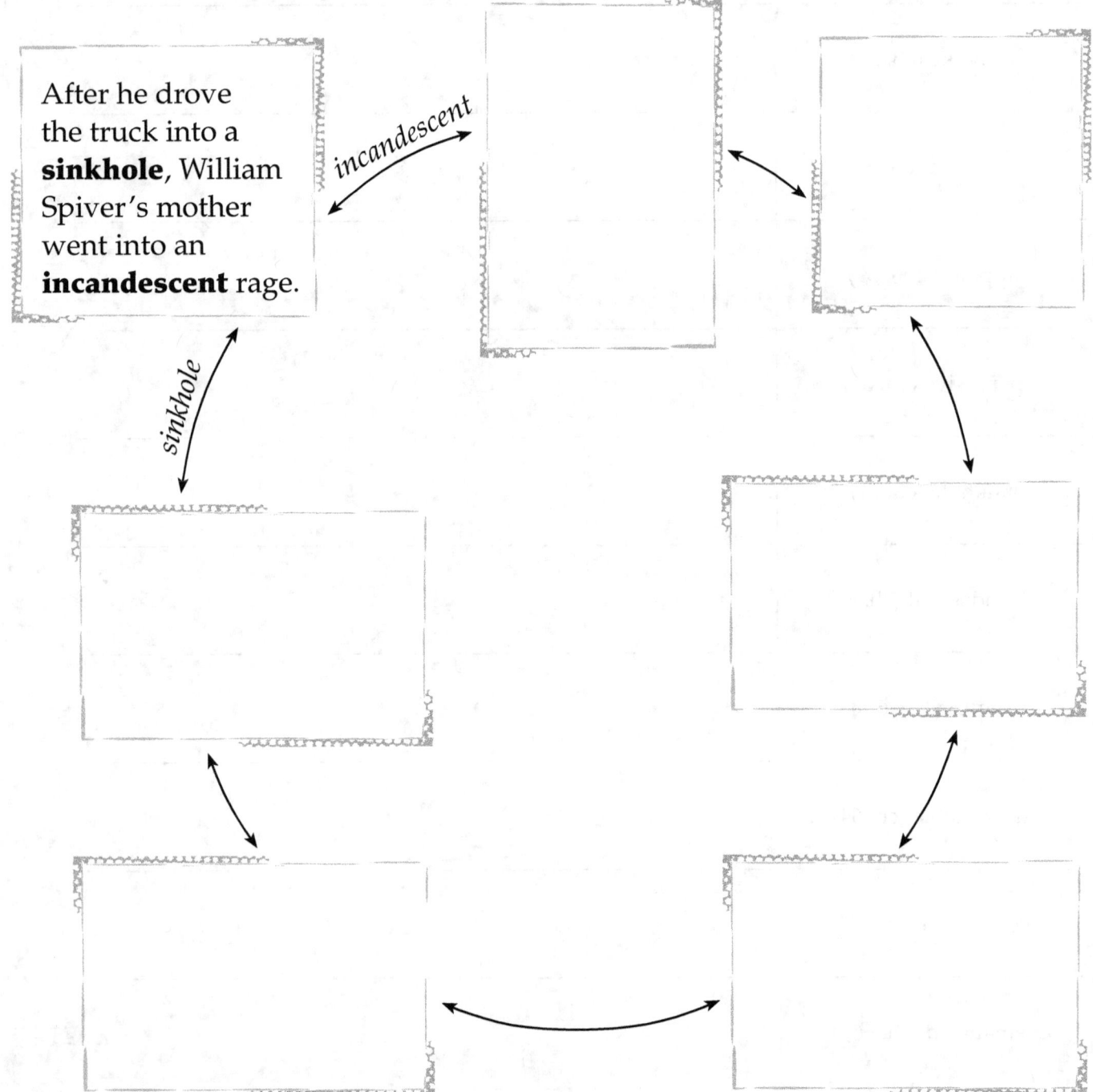

Teacher Plans—Section 5
Chapters 53–Epilogue

Analyzing the Literature

Provided below are discussion questions you can use in small groups, with the whole class, or for written assignments. Each question is given at two levels so you can choose the right question for each group of students. Activity sheets with these questions are provided (pages 58–59) if you want students to write their responses. For each question, a few key discussion points are provided for your reference.

Story Element	■ Level 1	▲ Level 2	Key Discussion Points
Character	Why does Phyllis Buckman's attempt to deceive her daughter fail so miserably?	In dictating the letter, how does Phyllis Buckman underestimate Flora's relationship with Ulysses?	The moment Flora reads the dictated letter, she knows that Ulysses didn't write it and that he's in trouble. She knows he would never sign anything "Mr. Squirrel" because that's not his name.
Plot	What does Flora dream of doing and what is the significance of her dream?	How is Flora's dream a form of foreshadowing?	Flora dreams of feeling happy while holding William Spiver's hand and later that evening, she actually does so as they are walking along the road. Against her cynical wishes, she is bonding with William, and the dream is one of her first clues.
Setting	How can you tell that Flora doesn't live in a city?	What kind of environment does Flora live in (urban, suburban, small town, or rural), and how do you know?	Flora probably lives in a small town or a suburb. Phyllis takes Ulysses into the woods, and when he escapes from her, he quickly finds the Giant Do-Nut sign and the Blixen Arms apartments. Also, when Flora, Tootie, and William are driving and walking around, they do not appear to be in an urban setting.
Character	What happens to alter Flora's relationship with her mother?	How does Flora's relationship with her mother change at the end of the story?	When Flora sees how distraught her mother is over the fact that her daughter was missing and also that she seems unfazed by Mary Ann being broken, Flora realizes that her mother loves her more than the lamp.

Chapters 53–Epilogue

Name _____

Date _____

Analyzing the Literature

Directions: Think about the section you just read. Read each question and state your response with textual evidence.

1. Why does Phyllis Buckman's attempt to deceive her daughter fail so miserably?

   _____
   _____
   _____
   _____
   _____

2. What does Flora dream of doing and what is the significance of her dream?

   _____
   _____
   _____
   _____
   _____

3. How can you tell that Flora doesn't live in a city?

   _____
   _____
   _____
   _____
   _____

4. What happens to alter Flora's relationship with her mother?

   _____
   _____
   _____
   _____
   _____

Name _____
Date _____

Chapters 53–Epilogue

▲ Analyzing the Literature

Directions: Think about the section you just read. Read each question and state your response with textual evidence.

1. In dictating the letter, how does Phyllis Buckman underestimate Flora's relationship with Ulysses?

   _____
   _____
   _____
   _____
   _____

2. How is Flora's dream a form of foreshadowing?

   _____
   _____
   _____
   _____
   _____

3. What kind of environment does Flora live in (urban, suburban, small town, or rural), and how do you know?

   _____
   _____
   _____
   _____
   _____

4. How does Flora's relationship with her mother change at the end of the story?

   _____
   _____
   _____
   _____

Chapters 53–Epilogue

Name _____

Date _____

Reader Response

Directions: Choose one of the following prompts about this section to answer. Be sure you include a topic sentence in your response, use textual evidence to support your opinion, and provide a strong conclusion that summarizes your opinion.

Writing Prompts

- **Narrative Piece**—If you were a character in this story, how would it affect the plot? Rewrite a scene from this section with you added to the scene.
- **Informative/Explanatory**—Consider Flora's mother's behavior in this section. If you were Flora, how would your mother behave about Ulysses and his superpowers? How would your mother behave if she couldn't find you in the house in the middle of the night?

_____
_____
_____
_____
_____
_____
_____
_____
_____
_____
_____
_____
_____

Name _____
Date _____

Chapters 53–Epilogue

Close Reading the Literature

Directions: Closely reread all of chapter 57. Read each question and then revisit the text to find evidence that supports your answer.

1. Why does Flora bring the lamp when she goes to wake up William Spiver?

   _____
   _____
   _____

2. Use the text to explain the difficulties that William Spiver has navigating the world.

   _____
   _____
   _____
   _____

3. How can you tell that Flora is frustrated by William's initial response? Cite text evidence.

   _____
   _____
   _____
   _____

4. What words appear above Tootie's head in the darkness? Why?

   _____
   _____
   _____
   _____

Chapters 53–Epilogue

Name _____

Date _____

Making Connections–Sinkholes

Directions: Tootie claims that William Spiver drove his stepfather's truck into a lake. William says it was really a sinkhole. Conduct research to answer the questions below.

1. What is a sinkhole?

   _____
   _____
   _____
   _____

2. How do sinkholes typically form?

   _____
   _____
   _____
   _____

3. In what places are sinkholes most likely to form?

   _____
   _____
   _____
   _____

4. Does it matter whether William Spiver drove the truck into a lake or a sinkhole? Why or why not?

   _____
   _____
   _____
   _____

Name _____

Date _____

Chapters 53–Epilogue

Creating with the Story Elements

Directions: Thinking about the story elements of character, setting, and plot in a novel is very important to understanding what is happening and why. Complete **one** of the following activities based on what you've read so far. Be creative and have fun!

Characters

Rate Tootie Tickham's performance as the leader of the rescue mission using a scale of 1 (low) to 5 (high). Think about her actions and in a paragraph, defend your response.

Setting

Write the scene that occurs when Phyllis returns from the woods to find Flora and Mary Ann missing.

Plot

Is Flora's plan to exchange Mary Ann for Ulysses a good one? Write an email to her explaining why it is or isn't. Support your reasoning with evidence from the book.

Post-Reading Activities

Name _____

Date _____

Post-Reading Theme Thoughts

Directions: Read each of the statements in the first column. Choose a main character from *Flora and Ulysses*. Think about that character's point of view. From that character's perspective, decide if the character would agree or disagree with the statements. Record the character's opinion by marking an X in Agree or Disagree for each statement. Explain your choices in the fourth column using text evidence.

Character I Chose: _____

Statement	Agree	Disagree	Explain Your Answer
Most superheroes are created as the result of a near-tragic accident.			
Comics are the most entertaining type of literature.			
It is not wise to feel hopeful.			
Sometimes it's not clear that parents love their children.			

Name _____

Date _____

Post-Reading Activities

Culminating Activity: Create a New Adventure!

Directions: Create a new adventure for Flora and Ulysses. Include some of the characters from this book and introduce at least one new character.

First, decide if your adventure will be written as:
- text and comic strips
- text only
- comic strips only

Plan your adventure carefully. You may want to make an outline or create a graphic organizer before you begin writing to get your ideas recorded. Decide which parts will be text and which parts will be comic strip panels. If you choose to use only comic strips to tell the story, plan carefully and draw your pictures clearly. Fill in the bursts below with exciting sound-effect words and add them to your comic strip.

Comprehension Assessment

Directions: Circle the best response to each question.

1. What is the meaning of the word *conjured* as it is used in the book?
    A. stalled for time
    B. refused to believe
    C. brought into one's mind
    D. turned into an arch-nemesis

2. Why is Flora able to save Ulysses after he is vacuumed?
    E. She recalls how The Amazing Incandesto did CPR on his parakeet.
    F. Her mother made her watch a video about how to do CPR.
    G. She's read every issue of TERRIBLE THINGS CAN HAPPEN TO YOU!
    H. Her father taught her how to do CPR when he lived with her.

3. Contrast what Flora feels and thinks at the beginning of the book to how she feels and thinks at the end of the book.

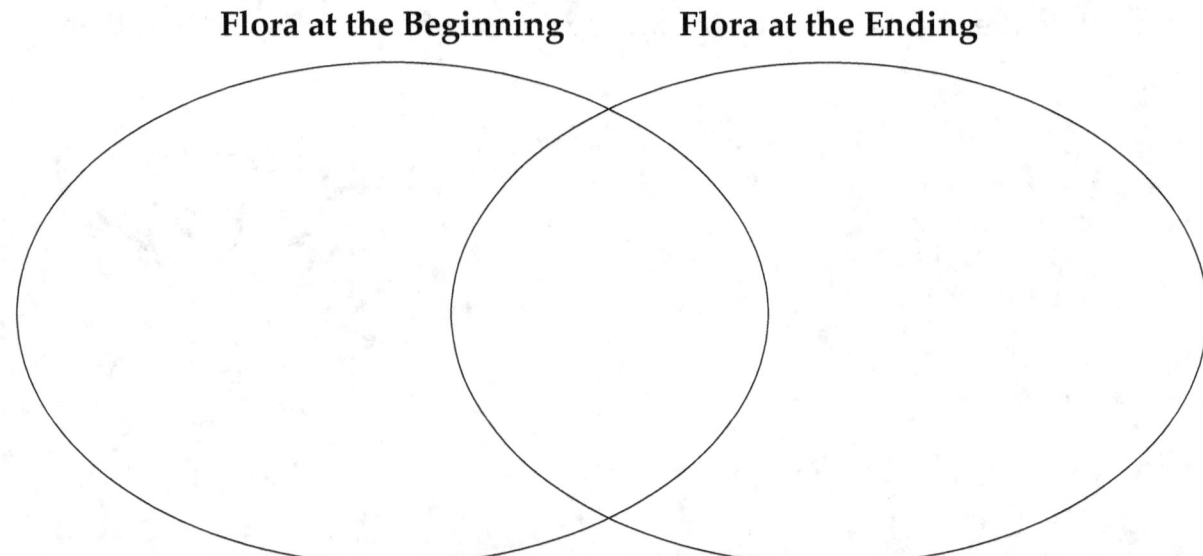

Flora at the Beginning   **Flora at the Ending**

4. Choose **two** supporting details that could be included in the diagram above.
    A. She decides to exchange Mary Ann for Ulysses.
    B. She is a cynic who doesn't care if her mother loves her or not.
    C. She wonders if people undress as they drive down the road.
    D. She tells Ulysses that she loves him.

Comprehension Assessment (cont.)

5. Why does Flora feel foreboding as her father drives her home?

   E. She fears the Dr. Meescham's giant squid painting will be hanging on the wall.

   F. She believes that William Spiver is in cahoots with her mother.

   G. She thinks her mother will refuse to let her live with her father.

   H. She knows that Ulysses's arch-nemesis is inside the house.

6. What quotation from the book provides the best evidence for your answer to number 5?

   A. "The giant squid is the loneliest of all God's creatures."

   B. "The only reason I am here, Flora Belle, is that I came looking for you."

   C. "Quit calling it the 'squirrel situation.' You asked him to murder my squirrel!"

   D. "Why did you say that your mother wanted a lamp for a daughter?"

7. What is the purpose of these sentences from the book:

   "My name is not now, nor has it ever been, nor will it ever be, Billy. I took issue with being so addressed. After repeatedly taking issue and repeatedly being ignored, one thing led to another and some irrevocable acts occurred. Thus, I was banished."

   _____

   _____

   _____

   _____

8. Which other quotation from the story serves a similar purpose?

   E. "My mother was incandescent with rage. I looked upon her rage and was blinded by disbelief and sorrow."

   F. "I promise to always turn back toward you."

   G. "'I wish my father were here,' said William Spiver."

   H. "Flora's heart, the lonely, many-armed squid of it, flipped and flailed inside of her."

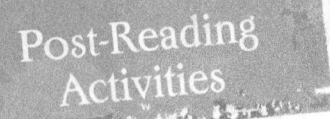

Name _____

Date _____

Response to Literature: Caring for an Exotic Pet

Flora intends to keep Ulysses. A squirrel is an exotic pet. In some states, it is illegal to own a pet squirrel. In others, it is legal as long as one possesses a wildlife permit. First, conduct research to determine if your state allows its citizens to keep pet squirrels. If your state does not allow pet squirrels, it may allow Siberian chipmunks. This breed of chipmunk has been domesticated, although they are still considered exotic pets. A sugar glider is another option for an exotic pet that is similar to a squirrel.

Directions: Based on what is legal in your state, research and prepare a visual presentation (*PowerPoint*, *Prezi*, etc.) describing how to care for a squirrel, a Siberian chipmunk, or a sugar glider. (If all three pets are legal in your location, choose whichever one you find most interesting.) Be sure to include housing, type of food, special considerations (such as can the animal be allowed outdoors and if so, in what kind of enclosure), and how to find an exotic veterinarian that will handle the animal's medical care. End your presentation with a statement of why you would or would not like to own this type of pet.

Vocabulary List

This list is included because part of the humor in this book relies on the use of words that are obscure and/or unusual for this reading level. Boldface words are included within the unit. The meaning of the * words can be ascertained from context clues.

multiterrain* (Introduction)
illuminated* (Introduction)
high jinks* (Introduction)
cynic (Introduction)
defiance (Introduction)
malfeasance (ch. 1)
cogitation* (ch. 1)
profound (ch. 2)
indomitable (ch. 3)
inadvertently (ch. 4)
obliged* (ch. 5)
submersion (ch. 8)
disdain (ch. 8)
smirk (ch. 10)
unassuming (ch. 10)
furrowed brow (ch. 11)
emblazoned (ch. 12)
absentminded (ch. 14)
idiocy (ch. 14)
stout (ch. 14)
emitting* (ch. 15)

installment (of comic) (ch. 15)
knell* (ch. 15)
hallucination (ch. 16)
plastered (ch. 16)
dictums (ch. 17)
distinguishes* (ch. 17)
trauma (ch. 17)
induced (ch. 17)
profoundly (ch. 17)
confines (ch. 17)
domestic (ch. 17)
spectacle (ch. 17)
rabid (ch. 17)
melodious (ch. 18)
treacherous (ch. 18)
anticlimactic (ch. 18)
retard (impede) (ch. 18)
cryptic (ch. 18)
positing* (ch. 18)
jest (ch. 18)
contraption (ch. 18)
suspended (ch. 19)

trance (ch. 19)
bestirred (ch. 20)
cold compress (ch. 21)
arch-nemesis (ch. 21)
scruff (ch. 21)
humane (ch. 23)
density (ch. 23)
mentor (ch. 25)
eradicate (ch. 25)
persistent (ch. 25)
escort (ch. 25)
neurotic (ch. 25)
hyperbole (ch. 25)
recitation (ch. 25)
ferocity (ch. 26)
obfuscation (ch. 26)
cahoots (ch. 26)
treachery (ch. 27)
nefarious (ch. 28)
surreptitiously (ch. 29)
junctures (ch. 29)
(with a) vengeance (ch. 29)
captivated (ch. 30)

Post-Reading Activities

Vocabulary List (cont.)

excessively* (ch. 33)
preternaturally (ch. 33)
slanderous (ch. 33)
hysteria (ch. 33)
concussion* (ch. 34)
ominous* (ch. 34)
imperative (ch. 34)
notorious (ch. 34)
incites (ch. 34)
facilitate (ch. 34)
accord (ch. 35)
perpetual (ch. 35)
facilitate (ch. 35)
mesmerizing (ch. 37)
assistance* (ch. 37)
euphemism* (ch. 37)
concussion* (ch. 37)
agitated* (ch. 37)
dilated (ch. 37)
amnesia* (ch. 37)
unremitting* (ch. 38)
conjured (ch. 38)
perspective (ch. 38)
inconsequential (ch. 38)
incisors (ch. 39)

capacious* (ch. 39)
vanquished* (ch. 40)
inordinately (ch. 40)
forestalled (ch. 41)
inanimate* (ch. 42)
foreboding (ch. 42)
palpable (ch. 42)
menace (ch. 42)
metaphorical (ch. 42)
eons (ch. 43)
festive (ch. 43)
loath (ch. 43)
treacle* (ch. 43)
redolent* (ch. 44)
treacherous (ch. 44)
euphemistically (ch. 44)
denounced (ch. 45)
persevere (ch. 45)
retract (ch. 45)
inept (ch. 45)
banished* (ch. 45)
manifestations (ch. 45)
appellation (ch. 48)
irrevocable (ch. 48)
fraught (ch. 48)
empathize (ch. 48)

heft (ch. 50)
coherence (ch. 50)
literally (ch. 51)
vehemently (ch. 51)
sentiments (ch. 51)
possessed* (ch. 51)
dybbuks (ch. 51)
jaded (ch. 51)
provoke (ch. 52)
dictation* (ch. 54)
depleted (ch. 55)
accessible (ch. 56)
appalled (ch. 59)
exhilarating (ch. 59)
symbolism (ch. 59)
pervasive (ch. 60)
sinkhole (ch. 61)
submerge (ch. 61)
incandescent (ch. 61)
monstrosity (ch. 61)
insomnia* (ch. 63)
insomniac* (ch. 63)
digress (ch. 63)
strewn (ch. 64)
inexplicable (ch. 64)
sepulchral (ch. 65)
emanated (ch. 66)

The responses provided here are just examples of what students may answer. Many accurate responses are possible for the questions throughout this unit.

During-Reading Vocabulary Activity—Section 1: Chapters 1–13 (page 16)

1. **Cogitation** is thinking. Typical squirrel **cogitation** isn't very deep, or **profound**; squirrels think only about food and avoiding enemies.
2. Both the Amazing Incandesto and Ulysses are superheroes, but they are **unassuming** because they do not seek praise or glory for their good deeds.

Close Reading the Literature—Section 1: Chapters 1–13 (page 21)

1. Flora's mother says, "Oh, she's beautiful; I love her with all my heart!"
2. Flora dislikes the lamp. She says, "You stupid lamp; mind your own business," and "If you're such a great shepherdess, where's the rest of your sheep?"
3. Flora is jealous of Mary Ann because "her mother never said that she was beautiful," and "She never said she loved Flora with all her heart."
4. She holds Ulysses carefully and realizes that he is warm.

Making Connections—Section 1: Chapters 1–13 (page 22)

CPR

1. CPR is done to preserve a person's brain function when the person is without a pulse or not breathing. The objective is to delay tissue death until medical help can take over.
2. This technique should be used when a person has a faint or no pulse or is not breathing or breathing erratically.
3. CPR steps:
   - Put person on his or her back.
   - Put the heel of your hand in the center of the person's chest; put your other hand on top.
   - Keep your elbows straight and use your upper body weight to push straight down hard. Do this about 100 times for each minute with rescue breaths.
   - Tilt the person's head back and lift his or her chin. Cover the person's mouth with your own and give two rescue breaths.
   - One cycle is 30 chest compressions followed by 2 breaths.
   - Continue doing CPR cycles until the person begins breathing or medical professionals arrive.
4. CPR has been successful if the person starts breathing on his or her own.

Heimlich Maneuver

1. The Heimlich maneuver is done to clear a person's airway when food or some other object blocks it. Without oxygen, permanent brain damage can occur in as little as 4 to 6 minutes.
2. Use the Heimlich maneuver when a person is choking and can't breathe.
3. Heimlich steps:
   - Position yourself behind the person and reach your arms around his or her waist.
   - Place your fist, thumb side in, just above the person's navel. Grab the fist tightly with your other hand.
   - Pull your fist abruptly upward and inward to increase airway pressure behind the obstructing object.
   - You may need to repeat the procedure several times before the object is dislodged.
   - Repeat the abdominal thrusts until the object is dislodged or medical professionals arrive.
4. The Heimlich maneuver is successful if the object comes out of the throat and the person can breathe.

During-Reading Vocabulary Activity—Section 2: Chapters 14–26 (page 26)

1. Phyllis is certain that Ulysses is **rabid** because he lost a lot of fur when he was vacuumed and because he's not acting like a typical wild squirrel.
2. Flora's doorbell **emits** an "angry, window-shattering, you-guessed-the-wrong-answer-on-a-game-show kind of buzz" that sounds like the electric chair.

Close Reading the Literature—Section 2: Chapters 14–26 (page 31)

1. William has an "extremely violent encounter with a shrub" that leaves him bleeding.
2. Flora's mom claps her hands and says, "How wonderful! A little friend for Flora." She also says, "Flora is very lonely and spends too much time reading comics."
3. Flora is not enthused about William and says, "I don't need a little friend."
4. Flora feels confident in stating that she's not strange since she's standing next to William Spiver who she refers to as "truly, profoundly strange."

Making Connections—Section 2: Chapters 14–26 (page 32)

Note: There is an entire book of poetry by Rainer Maria Rilke in the public domain located at: http://www.gutenberg.org/files/38594/38594-h/38594-h.htm

Close Reading the Literature—Section 3: Chapters 27–39 (page 41)

1. Dr. Meescham says that cynics are people afraid to believe. She wants Flora to believe in love and God and other good things, so she explains Pascal's wager to Flora. Pascal stated that since no one could prove God's existence, it was best to believe in God since one had everything to gain and nothing to lose.
2. She asks Dr. Meescham if she believes things, and Dr. Meescham responds, "There is much more beauty in the world if I believe things are possible." This makes Flora feel that it is safe to reveal that Ulysses is a superhero.
3. Dr. Meescham doesn't agree. She responds, "Who knows what he will do? Who knows whom he will save? So many miracles have not yet happened."
4. Dr. Meescham is an optimist who looks on the bright side all the time. She says, "All things are possible. In Blundermeecen, we expected the miraculous to happen. We knew it would come."

Answer Key

Making Connections—Section 3: Chapters 27–39 (page 42)

Insert the Punctuation Mark(s)	Tell Why You Chose It
1. "Help me!" screamed Rita.	Rita's voice shows excitement, so it needs an exclamation mark. Her statement needs a period.
2. Ernie and Rita work at the Giant Do-Nut.	This is a declarative statement.
3. "Ulysses!" Flora shouted to him.	Flora is shouting, which needs an exclamation mark. Her statement needs a period.
4. Is that a rabid animal?	The statement is a question.
5. "For the love of Pete, what's so funny?"	The statement is a question.
6. Get out of the way!	The statement shows excitement and needs an exclamation mark.
7. Dr. Meescham lives in the Blixen Arms building.	This is a declarative statement.
8. The giant squid is a lonely creature.	This is a declarative statement.
9. "Holy bagumba!"	The statement shows excitement and needs an exclamation mark.
10. Why does Flora slide off the horsehair sofa?	The statement is a question.

During-Reading Vocabulary Activity—Section 4: Chapters 40–52 (page 46)

1. Flora feels **foreboding** when she looks at her house because she knows her mother, Ulysses's arch-nemesis, is inside, and Flora fears what Phyllis will do to Ulysses.
2. William was **banished** from his home by his mother after he committed "irrevocable acts" against his stepfather.

Close Reading the Literature—Section 4: Chapters 40–52 (page 51)

1. Flora believes that her mother wants her to live with her father because Phyllis said, "Go ahead. It will make my life easier" when Flora said she wanted to move in with her dad. William disagrees and thinks that Phyllis only agreed to Flora's request because she was surprised and possibly hurt.
2. The word *banished* feels like a small, cold stone in the pit of Flora's stomach because she empathizes with William feeling unloved and sent away by his mother.
3. William Spiver's father was also named William, and he describes him as having great humility and intelligence. He could play the piano well and had an in-depth knowledge of the stars and astronomy.
4. The three things that most annoy William about Tyrone are: 1) he is unaware of the stars in the sky; 2) he sold William's father's piano; and 3) he insists on calling William "Billy" despite the fact that William repeatedly tells him to call him "William."

Close Reading the Literature—Section 5: Chapters 53–Epilogue (page 61)

1. Flora brings the lamp because she plans to offer Mary Ann to her mother in exchange for Ulysses's life.
2. William admits that even before he was blind, he was clumsy, although he says it as, "Things leap out of nowhere and bump into me."
3. Flora is clearly annoyed that William wants to put on his robe instead of rushing out the door to find Phyllis and Ulysses. She keeps interrupting him to say that it's an emergency and looks around for a stick to hit him over the head.
4. The words "Tootie to the rescue" appear above Tootie's head just as they would in a comic book because Flora is so glad that an adult is going to try to help her save Ulysses.

Making Connections—Section 5: Chapters 53–Epilogue (page 62)

1. A sinkhole is a depression or hole in the ground caused by a collapse of the ground's surface layer.
2. Sinkholes typically form in one of two ways: naturally or from land-use practices. The most common is that the rock underlying the land surface is limestone, carbonate rock, salt beds, or rocks that are dissolved by groundwater moving through them. A sinkhole is an area of ground that has no natural external surface drainage. New sinkholes can be caused by land-use practices, especially pumping groundwater and some construction practices. Sinkholes can also form when people change natural water-drainage patterns or new water-diversion systems are developed.
3. Sinkholes are most likely to form in karst landscapes, which cover about 10 percent of Earth's land. In the United States, sinkholes form most often in Florida.
4. It doesn't really matter whether William Spiver drove the truck into a lake or a sinkhole. Driving the truck into either one would cause extensive damage, perhaps even totaling the vehicle.

Comprehension Assessment (pages 66–67)

1. C. brought into one's mind
2. G. She's read every issue of *TERRIBLE THINGS CAN HAPPEN TO YOU!*
3. **Flora at the Beginning:** cynical, doesn't believe her parents love her, spends all her time alone reading comic books, doesn't dare to hope **Flora at the Ending:** believes her parents love her, is friends with William Spiver, has a superhero pet squirrel **Both:** smart, creative, funny
4. B. She is a cynic who doesn't care if her mother loves her or not. D. She tells Ulysses she loves him.
5. H. She knows that Ulysses's arch-nemesis is inside the house.
6. C. "Quit calling it the 'squirrel situation.' You asked him to murder my squirrel!"
7. These sentences describe why William lashed out against his stepfather, Tyrone, by destroying his truck, resulting in William being sent to live with his Great Aunt Tootie.
8. E. "My mother was incandescent with rage. I looked upon her rage and was blinded by disbelief and sorrow."

www.ingramcontent.com/pod-product-compliance
Lightning Source LLC
Chambersburg PA
CBHW051422070526
44584CB00023B/3542